AF345578

YHWH...To All Generations

21 Reflections of Worship & Adoration

Demetrius Wilson

BookLeaf
Publishing

India | USA | UK

Copyright © Demetrius Wilson
All Rights Reserved.

This book has been self-published with all reasonable efforts taken to make the material error-free by the author. No part of this book shall be used, reproduced in any manner whatsoever without written permission from the author, except in the case of brief quotations embodied in critical articles and reviews.

The Author of this book is solely responsible and liable for its content including but not limited to the views, representations, descriptions, statements, information, opinions, and references ["Content"]. The Content of this book shall not constitute or be construed or deemed to reflect the opinion or expression of the Publisher or Editor. Neither the Publisher nor Editor endorse or approve the Content of this book or guarantee the reliability, accuracy, or completeness of the Content published herein and do not make any representations or warranties of any kind, express or implied, including but not limited to the implied warranties of merchantability, fitness for a particular purpose.
The Publisher and Editor shall not be liable whatsoever...

Made with ♥ on the BookLeaf Publishing Platform
www.bookleafpub.in
www.bookleafpub.com

Dedication

This book is dedicated to the generations of those who came before who paved the way... to those yet to come, may the testimony and praise of Yahweh be upon their lips, and within their hearts always!

To the revelation at the wonder of our creator as revealed through the birth of my grandson and next generation...
Mr. Ioannis Wade Wilson!

Preface

The writer in **Psalm 145:4** declares that each generation that will the name of Yahweh to the next, and proclaim his deeds! This is just one verse among many that speak to the reality of how He is generational in his relationship with mankind. I am grateful that He is consistent in His love and kindness to us, in that we have the opportunity to see His mighty hand do miraculous wonders! The things that he has done are beyond our ability to ever comprehend. His works are marvelous, and are to be declared from one generation to the other.

The writings in this book are meant to encourage the reader to reflect on the goodness of Yahweh, and be reminded of His mighty deeds in your own life. May we ever rejoice in His greatness, and testify to each generation of His wonderous works!

Acknowledgements

I am grateful for the relationship that I have with Yahweh. His grace has allowed me to experience the blessing called family through my favorite people! Thank you Abba!

-My Wife-
Adrienne - Thank you for being my partner in life, and helping me raise great children.

-My Children-
Drake, Darriyon, & Dustyn

-The Next Generation-
Ioannis!

1. He's A Wonder

He is above all that has ever been known,
more than all of the greatness that has ever been shown,
His power is vast and on full display,
Creation declares His glory each day.

The King of glory, He reigns supreme,
The Most High, Our Father He is Elohim,
The praise of His majesty is all around,
His wisdom and honor is duly renowned.,

Merciful, just, faithful and true,
Glorious praises to Him ever due,
Mighty, holy, worthy, our king,
Ruler over everything!

He is the refreshing of the weary mind,
The hope of glory and joy divine,
When my life I begin to ponder,
I do declare in my soul He's a wonder!

2. Faithful & True

So faithful and true,

I will forever trust Him,

His promise is sure!

3. Marvelous Works

Elohim, has created the expanse of the universe,
And designed it as He willed,
He spoke into the void and chaos,
And every word was fulfilled!

His knowledge is unsearchable,
To his wisdom there is no end,
The works of His hands are evident,
Confounding the most brilliant of men!

What He has done could never be denied,
Yet, beyond our comprehension capacity,
Only by faith do we embrace the belief,
At His display of unyielding tenacity!

All of His works are marvels indeed,
They are the testament of unlimited ability,
They could never be fully described,
In all of the annuls of human history!

Whether roaring seas, or towering mountains,
All creation declares He is glorious,
Daily our eyes behold His artistry,
These are works so great and marvelous!

4. Generations Testify

Generations are telling the story,
Of the victories that have been won,
The words echo through the ages,
Saying, " Look what Yahweh has done".

Generations are singing with gladness,
Their tongues filled with jubilant praise,
They are proclaiming to all who will hear,
All about Yah, the ancient of days!

Generations are calling Him Rapha,
The healer of all manner of affliction,
As time and again He has proven,
That He is the great physician.

Generations are calling Him Yirah,
He has provided all that was needed,

He has been the source of all things,
Expectations of Him, far exceeded.

Generations will exclaim to the other,
As long as time shall unfold,
That Yahweh has been, and ever will be,
As He has been since days of old!

5. Do Tell

"Do tell", says the child with gleaming eyes,
"What happened?"

"Sit down little one" the aged one replies,
"I will tell you!"

"You must know dear child" says the aged one with
joyful tears.
"Yahweh did it!"

"Yes" says the aged one recalling many years.
"Not one time has he failed!"

"How" asks the little one with curiosity,
"Do tell me more!"

"Oh", says the aged one, "just His generosity"
"He is faithful!"

The little one responds, "I hope the same for me!"

"Do you think it will be?"

"No doubt" says the aged one, "It's a guarantee!"
"He will!"

6. I Pledge

My allegiance has been given only to the Most High,
I have chosen to live for Him.

My affection is for things above which cannot fade away,
I have chosen to pursue them.

My mind has been surrendered to His will and His ways,
I have chosen to obey His commands.

My life has been dedicated to accomplish what He
pleases,
I have chosen to put it all in His hands.

My attention has been captured by the power of His
Word,
I have chosen to be all in.

My heart has been set to hide His Word within it,
I have chosen to walk away from sin

I pledge allegiance to Yahweh... May He Reign Forever

7. He and Us

With love and kindness He draws us,
Despite our shortcomings He calls us,

Through His great mercy He graces us,
In great despair He braces us.

In times of trouble He hides us
Through great trials He guides us

In stormy seasons He holds us,
Through tribulation He molds us.

Through imperfection He teaches us,
In lowly places He reaches us.

Inside and out He knows us,
What we don't know He shows us.

HE IS FOR US!

8. True Story/Love Story

It's true, It's all true,
We are genuinely loved!

It's true, Its all true,
It flows from above.

It's true, It's all true,
Yeshua's life was given,

It's true, It's all true,
From the grave He has risen

It's true, It's all true,
He was punished for our sin

It's true, It's all true,
He's really coming back again.

It's true, It's all true,
The price of freedom has been paid,

It's true, It's all true,
There is now an empty grave.

It's true, It's all true,
Love is central to this story,

It's true, It's all true,
To the praise of His glory

9. A B B A

The Father has ... **Always Been**
the **Best Answer**

The Father will ... **Always Be** the
Best Answer

HE IS
The **Strength** of The House

10. Hope & Obey

We wait on the change,
as the atmosphere is so strange
As many boldly declare
Their struggle with healthcare
Broken promises of better things
One mourns as another sings
How confused some must be
My task is to bring clarity
I pray as you read you grasp
This vision that I must cast
Hope existed before time began
Before the creation of feeble man
There were no high courts to rule
no unjust government, harsh and cruel.

Before slavery, and evil Jim Crow
before the KKK so filthy and low
Hope was alive before it was known
Before the reality of things to own

Before racism or any notion of pride
Without any doubt hope was alive
True has been true real has been rea
l In due time hope is always revealed
Hope is not a what but really who
He must be the true anchor for you
Listen closely and don't be confused
Hoping in man only leaves you abused

Men cannot ever make us great again
Great equals repenting from our sin
Shema oh my people please understand
Return to obey Hope's every command
My people turn from froward ways
Come back and obey the Ancient of Days
Real hope endures and will never fade
Not just hype not a fleeting charade

Dark days are upon us many just ahead
Yet "The Light" has come Isaiah 60 said
Yes in Hope and light we must arise
Live in truth without compromise
Listen, study be instructed and obey
Do not be dull of hearing I pray
Your adversary comes to "slay everyday"
True Hope will keep him at bay..

Israel. Please just (hope) obey! -

11. Encouraged

I am tired but

determined to move forward

AND I will do this.

12. The Children

The children are our blessings,
Sent to us from the Father above,
They are full of life and innocence,
And remind us Yahweh's great love.

They are to be taught of His ways,
To be raised to reverence his name,
To be dedicated again in faith,
To the one from whence they came.

Never to be abandoned,
Harmed, hurt or abused,
They are to be cared for lovingly,
Lest they become confused,

They are great truly blessings,
They are like arrows of a mighty man,
When we raise them with grace and wisdom,

They are able to thrive in the land.

They are our seed and mighty in the earth,
As the promise to righteous ones,
They are our precious children,
Something special is in each one.

Boys and girls, locks and curls,
Smiles and wandering eyes,
Imagination, loads of energy,
Little laughs and little cries.

They belong to Yahweh,
Only to us on loan,
May we glorify The Father,
As we welcome them home.

13. A Father's Prayer

Father I do thank you,
That you have graced me for this task,
As I face each challenge,
For you wisdom I do ask.

Show me how to demonstrate,
The love you have for me,
Help me as I lead my children,
To be all that they should be.

Thanks for helping me grow,
As I become a better man,
Father they are depending on me,
So I'm holding to your hand.

Bless my children always,
May they always follow you,
May they see you on my life,
As you are their father too.

Thank you for their gifts,
May they use them for you,
May they growth in wisdom and stature,
And see your favor too.

Thank you for their protection,
Keep them on all of their ways,
And may we all follow after you,
The full balance of our days.

14. Wisdom

This is essential

It is the principal thing

There is but one source.

15. Dwelling Place

To be in this place with you is shalom,
What I find here could never be replaced,
It is where I long to be,
The is my dwelling place.

Fullness of joy and freedom,
Is my portion in your presence alone,
I humbled myself in adoration,
As I worship before your throne.

You have caused me to be satisfied,
In the bounty of your supply,
I have need of nothing,
As long as with you I abide.

HalleluYah! You are my dwelling place!

16. SHALOM

SHALOM

... chaos be done.

... victory be won!

... enemies be removed

... strength be renewed.

... sickness be healed

... promises fulfilled

SHALOM

17. Remember

Remember the hand of Yahweh
who has delivered us,

Remember His goodness forever
in His name we trust.

Remember He brings us justice
and He never leaves our side.

Remember that He is our comfort
His arms are open wide.

Remember that He has been gracious
His compassions never fail.

Remember He is our Salvation
He has made all things well.

18. L O V E

This is The Father

Revealed through us to others

We owe EVERYONE!

19. YHWH To All Generations

The same, always He will never change,
He ever lives in the strength of His name!

YHWH

Philosophies of man fail each passing day,
But His word will stand and not fade away!

YHWH

He is the ruler above every nation,
His truth ensures to all generations!

YHWH

20. J O Y

It's Unspeakable

AND it is full of glory

not given by the world!

21. Great Grace

True gift is great grace

We are empowered through it

Most beneficial

www.ingramcontent.com/pod-product-compliance
Lightning Source LLC
La Vergne TN
LVHW010021200726
843495LV00015B/1870